#BOOK TITLE **tweet**

140 Bite-Sized Ideas for Compelling Article, Book, and Event Titles

By Roger C. Parker
Foreword by Michael Larsen

First Printing: June 2010
Paperback ISBN: 978-1-61699-026-8 (1-61699-026-0)
eBook ISBN: 978-1-61699-027-5 (1-61699-027-9)
Place of Publication: Silicon Valley, California, USA
Paperback Library of Congress Number: 2010926576

Advance Praise

"It all starts with a title, and Roger Parker will get you started on that."

Jack Hart, author, 'A Writer's Coach'

"Successful titles attract attention, then tell prospects why to buy. After seeing how others have done it, you'll be able to do it yourself."

William Reed, author, speaker and creativity consultant; http://www.williamreed.jp

---

"Save yourself a lot of time and heartache; the right title is absolutely crucial for any book. Roger crams lots of info into a small canvas."

Shel Horowitz, award-winning author of 'Grassroots Marketing for Authors and Publishers' and co-author of 'Guerrilla Marketing Goes Green' and six other books; http://www.frugalmarketing.com

---

"Creating titles is an art, and well-crafted ones will 'nuggetize' and convey a lot of information in few words. Just like this book."

Peter Bowerman, author of 'The Well-Fed Writer'; http://www.wellfedwriter.com

---

"Crisp, hard hitting titles are crucial; they can make or break whatever you write. Get Roger's book to come up with the perfect title."

Mark Steisel, ghostwriter; http://www.marksteisel.com

"Any busy person who wants to write a book should make this book part of their reference collection—and start using it immediately."

Steve Atlas, author of 'Car Free at the Beach' and 'Single Parenting: a Practical Resource Guide' and creator of http://carfreeamerica.com and http://carfreeamerica.org

---

"Twitter helps writers to streamline their thoughts into 140 characters, so why not book titles? Learn how to make your title ReTweetable!"

Joanna Penn, author of 'Author 2.0'; http://www.thecreativepenn.com

---

"'#BOOK TITLE tweet' is a must-read for every author before they choose the all-important title for their book. It's hard to undo a bad title. '#BOOK TITLE tweet' will help you get the most from your book's title."

Tony Eldridge, coach and author, 'The Sampson Effect'; http://www.marketingtipsforauthors.com

Dedication

I dedicate this book to all subject area experts interested in sharing their knowledge and passion with others.

Acknowledgments

I want to start by thanking the authors whose titles provided the inspiration for the ideas and examples in this book.

Next, I want to thank the Happy About editorial team, Mitchell Levy, Rajesh Setty, and Liz Tadman, whose hard work made this book possible.

Finally, I want to thank Betsy, my wife, for her support, as well as those who read my early drafts and shared their comments and enthusiasm.

Why Did I Write This Book?

I wrote this book because titles provide the basis of an article's, book's, or event's success.

Titles communicate at a glance. They play a "make or break" role in the success of the message that follows.

Ill-considered, hastily-created, last-minute titles instantly torpedo the success of articles, nonfiction books, or events.

Weak titles can also undermine the effectiveness of your blog posts and emails (every subject line is a title) as is every Twitter.

In addition to attracting the right readers, titles can set your message apart from the competition and create the basis of lasting brands.

Titles have been good to me. They've provided the basis of a good life plus numerous exciting intellectual challenges and satisfactions.

In the following pages, I share what I know, so others can select the titles needed to create their own benefits and rewards.

Roger C. Parker

Contents

Foreword by Michael Larsen

From my 30-year perspective as a literary agent,
titles sell books.
Getting a book picked up is half the battle.
Browsers look at books for just seconds; titles help
determine if they're going to read further.
Roger's excellent, easy-to-read ideas will help
you come up with titles to excite agents, editors,
booksellers, the media, and book buyers.

Michael Larsen

Michael Larsen is a partner in Larsen-Pomada,
Northern California's oldest literary agency,
http://www.larsen-pomada.com. He's also the author
of 'How to Write a Book Proposal' and 'How to Get
a Literary Agent,' and co-author, with Jay Conrad
Levinson, Rick Frishman, and David Hancock, of
'Guerrilla Marketing for Writers: 100 Weapons for
Selling Your Work.'

140 Bite-Sized Ideas for Compelling Article, Book, and Event Titles

Introduction

Why a Book About Titles—and Why Me?

Titles sell books the same way headlines in advertisements sell products and services; they *make a promise* that *compels further reading*.

Titles attract both readers and search engines. Without compelling titles, it's unlikely prospects will read your message.

Your titles must *sell at a glance*: they have to immediately convince busy readers to take the time to read the words that follow.

Twitter's 140-character format provides great training for creating brief, compelling titles that engage readers and prompt action.

Today, titles are even more important because they must appeal to search engines that will drive Internet traffic to your book and website.

I love titles; I've been analyzing the characteristics of titles that create strong brands for over 20 years.

My goal is to help you choose a title that makes an irresistible offer to your intended market and sets your book apart from the competition.

I want to help you choose a title that will create a powerful brand for both you and your book.

Section I

Characteristics of Successful Titles

Familiarize yourself with 16 typical characteristics usually found in successful titles.

1

Successful titles offer a promise, or benefit, that your intended readers desperately want, e.g., 'Get Clients Now!'

2

Target your readers by identifying whom you're writing for, e.g., 'Red Wine for Dummies.'

3

You can also position your topic by making it obvious whom you are not writing for, e.g., 'Design for Non-Designers.'

4

Focus on your prospect's desired results, e.g., 'Lose 21 Pounds in 21 Days.'

5

Use alliteration (repeated "hard" sounds) to make your title resonate in the reader's mind, e.g., 'Driven to Distraction.'

6

Relate your book to a famous role model, e.g., 'Innovate Like Edison: The Five-Step System for Breakthrough Business Success.'

7

Numbers add credibility to your title's promise, e.g., '1,000 Recordings to Hear Before You Die.'

8

If appropriate, make your title memorable by pushing the boundaries of good taste: 'The Toilet Paper Entrepreneur.'

9

Combine a short title with a longer subtitle that adds detail, e.g., 'Writing Tools: 50 Essential Strategies for Every Writer.'

10

Use titles beginning with action verbs, words ending in "ing," to imply a process, e.g., 'Looking Good in Print.'

11

Command readers to act by beginning titles with imperative verbs, e.g., 'Book Yourself Solid!' or 'Sell Your Book on Amazon.'

12

Titles should contain the keywords that readers use when searching for information, e.g., 'Writing White Papers.'

13

Spark reader curiosity with titles that are either contradictions in terms or exaggerations, e.g., 'The 4-Hour Workweek.'

14

Use metaphors to make your title's promise easily understood, e.g., 'The Well-Fed Writer' or 'Chicken Soup for the Pet Owner's Soul.'

15

Stress the reader's goal using a minimum number of words, e.g., 'Aiming at Amazon' or 'Sell Your Book on Amazon.'

16

Choose titles that promise complete information, e.g., 'The Copywriter's Handbook' or 'Encyclopedia of Natural Medicine.'

Section II

Examples and Best Practices

Examples and best practices illustrate ways you can use the ideas introduced in Section I.

17

Offer a specific number of solutions, e.g., 'Fifty Simple Ways to Live a Longer Life.'

18

Use a familiar word to indicate a fresh approach to a title, e.g., 'Management Rewired.'

19

Express the promise in familiar, conversational language, e.g., 'Getting to Yes: Negotiating Agreement Without Giving In.'

20

When possible, use words of equal length, e.g., 'Words That Work.'

21

Combine a promise title with a subtitle that provides more information, e.g., 'Made to Stick: Why Some Ideas Survive and Others Die.'

22

Opposites attract in titles, e.g., 'Smart Women/Foolish Choices: Finding the Right Man While Avoiding the Wrong Ones.'

23

Engage readers with the unexpected or unusual, e.g., 'The Black Swan' or 'The Purple Cow.'

24

Add rhythm to your titles, e.g., 'Buy*Ology: Why We Buy What We Buy.' Note the repetition of the word *buy*.

25

Relate your title to a familiar phrase, e.g., 'Emotional Intelligence: Why It Can Matter More Than IQ.'

26

Tell, then explain: 'The One-Page Proposal: How to Get Your Business Pitch onto One Persuasive Page.'

27

Start your titles with numbers; they simplify and add landmarks for readers, e.g., 'The 7 Habits of Highly Effective People.'

28

Add "latest information"
appeal to your titles, e.g., 'The
New Rules of Marketing &
PR' or 'The New Influencers.'

29

Make big goals appear easy to achieve by breaking them into a series of steps, e.g., '6 Steps to Take Your Marriage from Good to Great.'

30

Use your titles to show how quickly readers can benefit from your ideas, e.g., 'Guerrilla Marketing in 30 Days.'

31

Engage prospective readers by making them ask, "How can this be?" e.g., 'The Wealthy Barber.' After all, "How can a barber be wealthy?"

32

Build titles on familiar phrases—this makes them easier to understand and remember. "Go-getter," for example, becomes 'The Go-Giver.'

33

Create a new, but easily recognized, vocabulary, e.g., 'Buy*ology—Proof and Lies About Why We Buy.'

34

Use familiar, emotional words, e.g., 'In Sickness and In Health: How to Discuss and Create a Plan for Long-Term Care.'

35

Target your title to a specific circumstance, e.g., 'How to Sell When Nobody's Buying.'

36

Engage reader curiosity by playing with words, e.g., 'Predictably Irrational.'

37

Short titles permit large type on the cover, but always add an explanatory subtitle, e.g., 'Sway: The Irresistible Pull of Irrational Behavior.'

38

Position your book by projecting an "attitude,"— 'Mad Scam: Kick-Ass Advertising Without the Madison Avenue Price Tag.'

39

Emphasize how little work is required, e.g., 'Three Steps to Yes.'

40

Include SEO keywords in your title and subtitle, e.g., 'The Business Startup Checklist and Planning Guide: Seize Your Entrepreneurial Dreams!'

41

Target your book to a specific market and situation, e.g., 'First Impressions: Creating Wow Experiences in Your Church.'

42

Project optimism, e.g., 'How to Get Happily Published.' The same content with a negative title might not have sold over 500,000 copies!

43

Position your book to appeal to the way readers think about the topic, e.g., 'The Pay As You Go Business Planning Book.'

44

Promise to focus on just the most important ideas, e.g., 'The Essential Don Murray: Lessons from America's Greatest Writing Teacher.'

45

Choose titles that sound like readers talking—then explain; 'Now All We Need is a Title: Famous Book Titles and How They Got That Way.'

46

Make the benefit transparently obvious, e.g., 'Endless Referrals' or 'Customers for Life.'

47

Arouse curiosity with a contrarian title—one that goes against conventional thinking, e.g., 'Goal-Free Living: How to Have the Life You Want Now!'

48

Show your readers where you're going to take them, e.g., 'From Entrepreneur to Infopreneur.'

49

Target your readers by identifying their situation, e.g., 'The Single Mother's Survival Guide.'

50

Reflect reader attitudes, e.g., 'Skinny Bitch: A No-Nonsense Guide for Savvy Girls Who Want to Stop Eating Crap and Start Looking Fabulous.'

51

Use imperative verbs plus an exclamation point to add urgency, e.g., 'Drive to Survive!'

52

Describe the tools your book offers, e.g., 'Helping Your Angry Child: Worksheets, Fun Puzzles, & Engaging Games to Help You Communicate Better.'

53

Emphasize quick results, e.g., '30-Minute Meals' or 'How to Sell Your Home in 5 Days.'

54

Emphasize the number of ideas in your book, e.g., '1001 Ways to Market Your Books.'

55

Target specific experience and knowledge levels, e.g., 'Fundamentals of Nursing' or 'Advanced Marathoning.'

56

Target those who desire a specific type of goal, e.g., 'Selling to Big Companies.'

57

Shield your readers from possible embarrassment, e.g., 'Never Be Boring Again!'

58

Target readers seeking a specific approach to solve a problem or achieve a goal, e.g., 'Prevent & Treat Cancer with Natural Medicine.'

59

Compare the power of a specific title like 'Sell Your Book on Amazon' with a less specific title like 'Sell Your Book Online.'

60

Compare the power of a specific title like 'The One-Page Proposal' versus a broader title like 'Short Proposals that Work.'

61

Create a brand by giving yourself a nickname, e.g., 'Grammar Girl's Quick & Dirty Tips for Better Writing.'

62

Use a metaphor to describe your approach to achieving a goal, e.g., 'Presentation Zen.'

63

Book titles can never be too simple or too obvious, e.g., 'How to Write a Book Proposal' or 'How to Get a Literary Agent.'

64

Use the minimum number of words necessary to explain what your book is about, e.g., 'Content Strategy for the Web.'

65

Promise an "insider" look at your topic, e.g., 'Confessions of an Advertising Man,' or 'Publishing Confidential.'

66

Reference a familiar theme in your title, e.g., 'Four Seasons: The Story of a Business Philosophy' or 'Four Seasons of a Marriage.'

67

Base your title on an "if/then" structure, e.g., 'Think & Grow Rich' or 'Speak & Grow Rich.'

68

Choose titles that encourage your readers to dream, e.g., 'Coaching Millions' or 'Million Dollar Consulting.'

69

Promise mastery of a specific task, e.g., 'Landing Page Optimization.'

70

Emphasize the practicality of your approach, e.g., 'Search Engine Optimization: An Hour a Day.'

71

Emphasize your underlying philosophy as well as the promise, e.g., 'Letting Go of the Words: Writing Web Content that Works.'

Section III

Combining Title Techniques

Whenever possible, employ two or
more characteristics in a title.

72

Promise a complete solution to a specific market while identifying your approach, e.g., 'The Complete Psychotherapy Treatment Planner for Adults.'

73

Target a specific type of reader and specify exactly what you're offering, e.g., '101 Things To Do With Your Private Pilot's License.'

74

Use familiar words, then explain, e.g., 'Looking Good in Print: A Guide to Basic Design for Desktop Publishing.'

75

Issue an engaging command and explain it, e.g., 'Don't Make Me Think: A Common Sense Approach to Web Usability.'

76

Partner with a popular brand, e.g., 'Snoopy's Guide to the Writing Life.'

77

Use specifics to target a metaphor, e.g., 'The Dirt-Cheap Green Thumb: 400 Thrifty Tips for Saving Money, Time and Resources as You Garden.'

78

Target newcomers, there's always more of them than experienced users, e.g., 'The Complete Idiot's Guide to Getting Published.'

79

Create a new vocabulary and explain it in short, everyday words, e.g., 'Outliers: The Story of Success.'

80

Use a single meaningful modifier and emphasize what won't take place, e.g., 'How to Make Real Money Selling Books (Without Worrying about Returns).'

81

Emphasize your qualifications in the title, e.g., 'A Writer's Coach: An Editor's Guide to Words that Work.'

82

Indicate an updated edition of a book that added a new cultural term, e.g., 'Information Anxiety 2.'

83

Ask a question while stressing your unique qualifications, e.g., 'What Can a Dentist Teach You about Business, Life, & Success?'

84

Combine a promise with a specific plan, e.g., 'The Shortest Distance between You and a Published Book: 20 Steps to Success.'

Section IV

Leverage Your Title's Initial
Success into Future Success

Successful titles create lasting
brands you can easily adapt for future
endeavors and projects.

85

Follow up your initial success with versions targeting specific markets or problems, e.g., 'Guerrilla Marketing for Financial Advisors.'

86

Focus follow-up books on specific tools, e.g., 'Guerrilla Marketing Online.'

87

Create workbooks to complement your original book, e.g., 'The 7 Habits of Highly Effective People Personal Workbook.'

88

Focus later books on specific circumstances, e.g., 'Guerrilla Marketing during Tough Times.'

89

Use the same tone, e.g., 'Skinny Bitch in the Kitch: Kick-Ass Recipes for Hungry Girls Who Want to Stop Cooking Crap (and Start Looking Hot!).'

90

Provide needed tools in your follow-up book, e.g., 'Guerrilla Marketing in 30 Days Workbook.'

91

Take your readers to the next level, e.g., follow 'Book Yourself Solid' with 'Beyond Booked Solid.'

92

Promise more information than your previous book, e.g., 'More Guerrilla Marketing Research.'

93

Use the same theme and structure in later titles: Jim Collins followed 'Good to Great' with 'Built to Last' and 'How the Mighty Fall.'

94

Adapt your title to a specific age group, e.g., 'What Color Is Your Parachute for Retirement?' or 'The 7 Habits of Highly Effective Teens.'

95

Indicate a fresh look at your previous book, e.g., 'The E-Myth Revisited.'

96

Add a year to update your earlier edition, e.g., 'Cooking for Two: 2009, The Year's Best Recipes Cut Down to Size.'

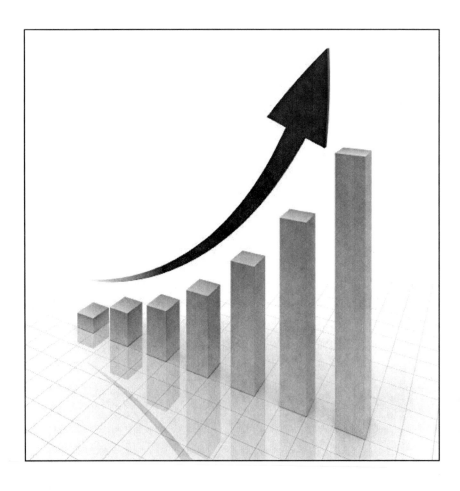

Section V

20 Quick & Easy Title Template Ideas

Start creating your title by using the following "fill in the blank" suggestions.

97

_____ and ____. (Do this) and (here's how you'll benefit), e.g., 'Speak and Grow Rich' or 'Think and Grow Rich.'

98

_____ when _____. (What to do) when (this symptom is present), e.g., 'What to Expect When You're Expecting.'

99

Understanding _____,
Understanding (topic, goal,
or task), e.g., 'Understanding
Wood Finishing: How
to Select and Apply
the Right Finish.'

100

Understanding your _____,
(task or goal),
e.g., 'Understanding Your
Health' or 'Understanding
and Changing Your
Management Style.'

101

Inside a/the _____ (occupation or situation), e.g., 'Inside the Painter's Studio.'

102

How to Avoid _____ (negative scenario or event), e.g., 'How to Avoid Probate' and 'How to Avoid Falling in Love with a Jerk.'

103

How to Avoid _____ with _____ (describe way to avoid negative event), e.g., 'How to Avoid Probate with a Revocable Living Trust.'

104

How to _____ (solve problem or achieve goal), e.g., 'How to Survive Anywhere' or 'How to Speak to Anyone.'

105

_____ Steps to _____, (solve problem or achieve goal), e.g., 'Six Steps to Free Publicity' or '7 Steps to a Pain-Free Life.'

106

The _____ (your name or term) Principle, e.g., 'The 80/20 Principle: The Secret to Success by Achieving More with Less.'

107

_____ Principles of _____
(task or problem to be
solved), e.g., 'The 7 Principles
of Making a Marriage Work.'

108

The _____ (task to be performed) Handbook, e.g., 'The Copywriter's Handbook' or 'The Feeling Good Handbook.'

109

Secrets of _____ (task or problem), e.g., 'The Presentation Secrets of Steve Jobs: How to Be Insanely Great in Front of Any Audience.'

110

_____ Ways to _____ (solve problem, achieve goal), e.g., '99 Ways to Get Kids to Love Writing' or '101 Ways to Make Every Second Count.'

111

The _____ Companion, e.g., 'The Knitter's Companion' or 'The Wine Lover's Companion.'

112

_____ (goal) that _____, (promise), e.g., 'Book Proposals that Sell: 21 Secrets to Speed Your Success.'

113

_____ (goal or task) for _____, (situation), e.g., 'Cooking for Two: Perfect Meals for Pairs.'

114

_____ (activity) into _____ (desired change), e.g., 'Coaching Sales Professionals into Sales Champions.'

115

_____ (goal): _____,
(approach to achieving it),
e.g., 'Endless Referrals:
Network Your Everyday
Contacts into Sales.'

116

_____ (goal) Like _____, (example), e.g., 'Build Like a Pro: Trim Carpentry,' 'Think like Leonardo DaVinci,' or 'Think Like Your Customer.'

Section VI

Steps to Title Success

A five-step foundation that can focus your thinking towards brainstorming possible titles.

117

Research titles used by other authors in your field. Look for a correlation between sales rank and title.

118

Identify the readers you most want to buy your book. Look for readers like your best clients. List their shared problems and goals.

119

Describe the promise, or the change, your book will help them obtain. Identify the steps needed for readers to achieve their desired change.

120

Distill the proposed title down to the shortest words that describe your book as emotionally as possible.

121

Never trust your instinct.
Test your book's proposed
title before using it. Create a
simple online survey to get
readers' opinions.

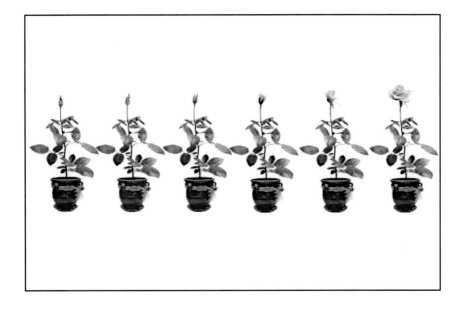

Section VII

Research Tips

One of the best ways to create a winning title is to analyze and apply ideas you see in existing titles.

122

Study headlines on magazine covers. Book titles, like magazine headlines, must grab readers' attention and engage their interest.

123

When analyzing "specificity" titles containing numbers, notice how much less effective they would be without the numbers.

124

When searching online for book title ideas, be sure to search for ideas at used and out-of-print book sellers, like http://www.alibris.com.

125

Keep track of your title ideas using worksheets printed on 3-hole paper that you save in a 3-ring binder.

126

Explore best-selling titles organized by category at Amazon.com, e.g., *Books > Science > Nature & Ecology > Natural Resources.*

Section VIII

Survey Tips

Never trust intuition or opinion;
instead, test the effectiveness
of your title ideas.

127

Use a checklist, like the one

at http://tinyurl.com/12titlecha,[1]

to rate how well your title

satisfies the 12 important

title characteristics.

---

1. www.publishedandprofitable.com/public/92.cfm

128

Ask yourself if your proposed
title contains the keywords
you've found to attract the
most qualified web traffic.

129

Read your titles out loud; if they're not easy for you to say, they won't be easy for readers to read and remember.

130

Memorable, descriptive titles, like 'Presentation Zen,' pave the way for follow-up books like 'Presentation Zen Design.'

131

Only authors with a strong following in a narrow niche can get by with a simple, descriptive title like 'Eyetracking Web Usability.'

132

Never test just one title. Instead, offer a choice of two or three titles.

133

Always invite survey participants to offer their own title and subtitle suggestions if they desire.

134

Separate titles and subtitles in surveys; let participants select their favorite title in Question 1 and their favorite subtitle in Question 2.

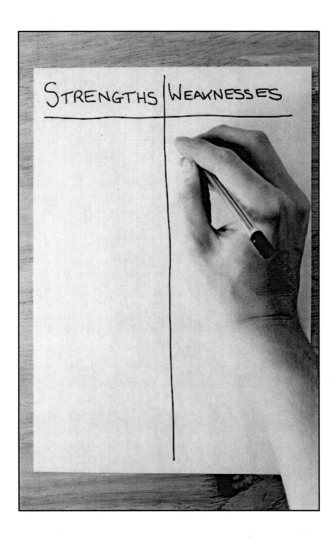

Section IX

Conclusion—A Word of Caution

Why successful titles are not enough, and a few other pointers.

135

Titles are powerful; they can attract attention, engage prospects, and pave the way to profitable relationships and sales.

136

But, and it's a "big but," your contents must live up to the promise you made in your title.

137

If your article, book, or event fails to live up to the promise you made in the title, you've lost all possibilities of future sales.

138

You can position a book by subtly flattering the intelligence of your intended readers, e.g., 'The Savvy Author's Guide to Book Publicity.'

139

Mix words in popular phrases, like *it's not rocket science* or *it's not brain surgery*, to create a new title, e.g., 'Rocket Surgery Made Easy.'

140

Before you press *Print* or *Send*, ask yourself: *Does my content live up to the title?* If it doesn't, you could do lasting damage to your brand.

Section X

Resources

Suggestions for further reading
and online research.

Books

Horn, Sam. 'POP! Create the Perfect Pitch, Title, and Tagline for Anything.' Tips for choosing titles that resonate in your reader's mind.

Bernard, Andre. 'Now All We Need is a Title: Famous Book Titles and How They Got That Way.' Entertaining anecdotes about bungled first tries.

Covert, Jack and Sattersten, Todd. 'The 100 Best Business Books of All Time: What They Say, Why They Matter, and How They Can Help You.' Study what's worked for others.

Gorman, Tom. 'Writing the Breakthrough Business Book: The Ultimate Guide for Consultants, Entrepreneurs, Executives, Experts and Writers.'

Online

Bestseller Lists, 1900-1995.
Search yearly lists of fiction and
nonfiction bestsellers for shared title
characteristics.
http://tinyurl.com/y87bdm9. [2]

'10 years of best sellers: How the
landscape has changed.' *USA Today*
article written by Bob Minzesheimer.
http://tinyurl.com/ydylyfj[3]

---

2.   www.caderbooks.com/bestintro.html
3.   www.usatoday.com/life/books/news/2004-03-10-
     bookslist-decade-main_x.htm

Bear, John. 'The Number One New York Times Best Seller.' Entertaining study of 484 books that have been #1 New York Times bestsellers. Out of print; available used at http://www.alibris.com.

Visit http://www.surveymonkey.com to learn how to create email and online title surveys for free.

When you need a synonym for a long word, visit http://www.thesaurus.com.

Search for inspiration at Bartlett's Familiar Quotations online at http://www.bartleby.com.

About the Author

Roger C. Parker is a best-selling and book coach. He helps authors plan, write, promote, and profit from books that build brands.

Learn more at http://www.publishedandprofitable.com, where you'll find over 500 pages of resources, interviews, templates, and worksheets.

Sign up to receive daily writing tips at Roger's *Published & Profitable* blog at http://blog.publishedandprofitable.com and the Book Title Tips blog at http://www.booktitletips.com.

You can find bonus titles and free Title Planning and Evaluation Worksheets at the Book Title Resource Center, http://tinyurl.com/TitleResources. 4

---

4.   www.publishedandprofitable.com/public/674.cfm

More Advance Praise

"Picking out the right title for your book might be the difference between a best-seller and a flop. Follow Roger's advice and you'll be on the path to a best-selling title!"

Ryan Lee, author and Internet Entrepreneur;
http://www.ryanlee.com

"This is a great idea. Given that I'm currently going through the mental gymnastics of trying to name a book, I found the examples useful and the ideas inspired. With the growth in self-publishing, I expect we'll begin to see a lot of books that adopt the tactics and formulas that you propose here."

Paul Gillin, blogger and author of 'The New Influencers' and 'Secrets of Social Media Marketing'; http://gillin.com

---

"'#BOOK TITLE tweet' gift-wraps your passion with words that dance in your readers' heads—a new, indispensable tool for writers at any level."

Dr. Charles Parker, Predictable Solutions for ADHD Medications, http://www.corepsychblog.com

---

"I definitely recommend this fresh look at book titles to all my Guerrillas; filled with concise, relevant ideas and examples."

Jay Conrad Levinson, father of 'Guerrilla Marketing,' the world's best-selling marketing book series;
http://www.gmarketing.com

"As a direct response copywriter, I can tell you firsthand how crucial headlines are to the success of a business owner's marketing materials. And since titles are, basically, headlines for articles, book, or blog posts, they too must be powerful and engaging enough to generate immediate interest from the reader. This book includes so many ways to come up with clear and concise, powerful titles that it's a 'must read' for any business owner or marketer who needs engaging titles and content."

Merrill Clark, author of 'How Your Local Small Business Can Get More Customers On The Internet';
http://www.crestviewmarketing.com

"Concise, focused, thought-provoking. Helps avoid tunnel vision. Supports breaking out of the blank state that can occur when thinking alone."

Gary Monti, Center for Managing Change;
http://www.ctrchg.com

"If you love Twitter, you'll love Roger C. Parker's 140 bite-size ideas for book titles! Inspirational!"

Carolyn Howard Johnson, author of the 'How To Do It Frugally' series for writers;
http://www.HowToDoItFrugally.com

"Roger again displays his talent for combining opposites: theory with detail, broad topic with succinct writing, advice with friendliness."

Paul Swift, Editor Emeritus, 'Newsletter on Newsletters'

"The short, tweet-like character of the entries makes it a quick, easy-to-use checklist for authors seeking to develop titles that sell."

Phyllis Zimbler Miller, book coach and co-founder of Miller Mosaic Power Marketing;
http://www.MillerMosaicPowerMarketing.com

"Most people think titles are random thoughts or the publisher's responsibility. Roger's explanation of a title process helped me a lot."

Peter Zawistowski, author of 'Moody Like Me'

"At last! A book that addresses the biggest challenge for writers: finding the right title. Two big thumbs up!"

Stephanie Chandler, author of 'From Entrepreneur to Infopreneur'; http://www.stephaniechandler.com

---

"In his latest book, Roger C. Parker, the king of concise, once again proves he practices what he preaches."

John Lawlor, Host and Producer of 'Open Heart Talk Radio'; http://OpenHeartTalk.com

---

"A MUST HAVE! Who wants to create a million dollar book title? If it's you, Marketing Coach, Roger Parker's '#BOOK TITLE tweet' will not let you down. Anytime you can get decades of experience neatly packed inside a little, easy to read book, GRAB IT!"

Annie Jennings, National Publicity Strategist, Annie Jennings PR; http://www.AnnieJenningsPR.com

Breinigsville, PA USA
06 June 2010
239326BV00004B/3/P